DISCARDED

Le Conte's Report on
East Florida

FTU Monograph No. 1

John Eatton Le Conte
(Le Conte–Furman Collection)
(Photograph courtesy of Mrs. Charles H. McMillan,
St. Simons Island, Georgia.)

Le Conte's Report on East Florida

Edited by
Richard Adicks

A Florida Technological University Book
Orlando / 1978

The University Presses of Florida

The University Presses of Florida is the scholarly publishing
agency for the State University System of Florida

Copyright © 1978 by the Board of Regents
of the State of Florida

Typography and Printing by Storter Printing Company
Gainesville, Florida

Library of Congress Cataloging in Publication Data

Le Conte, John Eatton, 1784–1860.
   Le Conte's Report on East Florida.

   Corr. version of the 1822 ms. found in Record Group 77,
File 38 of the Records of the Office of the Chief of
Engineers in the National Archives under title:
Observations on the soil and climate of East Florida.
   Bibliography: p.
   1. Florida—Description and travel—To 1865.
I. Title. II. Title: Report on East Florida.
F315.L42   917.59'04'4   77-9286
ISBN 0-8130-0588-4

Contents

Preface	vii
Introduction	1
Observations on the Soil and Climate of East Florida	17
Notes	39
Bibliography	53
Selected List of Maps	61
Maps	67
Index	73

Preface

HE HOLOGRAPH of John Eatton Le Conte's report on Florida is in Record Group 77, File 38, of the Records of the Office of the Chief of Engineers in the National Archives. On a cover page, in Le Conte's hand, appears the title "Observations on the Soil and Climate of East Florida," with his signature, "John Le Conte, Capt. U.S. Army," and the date, "February & March 1822." In another hand the description is repeated: "Capt. Le Conte's Report on the Soil and Climate of Florida, February & March, 1822."

The report proper consists of twenty pages, written on both sides of the sheets and numbered 3 to 22. Pages 23 and 24 are a list of thermometer readings taken between February 10 and March 14.

For the sake of clarity, I have without noting it emended the text to correct misspellings (e.g., "untill" and "percieve") and to make the punctuation consistent, as, for example, where the change of a comma to a period would remove ambiguity. I have, of course, retained Le

Conte's spellings of place names, as well as his capitalization.

The parenthetical numbers in my introduction and notes refer to titles with corresponding numbers in the Bibliography.

I am grateful to Carol Shehadeh for initially transcribing Le Conte's manuscript; to Professors Haven Sweet, Henry Whittier, and William Oelfke of Florida Technological University for their help in identifying some of the plant life and other phenomena that Le Conte observed; to Sheldon Dobkin of the University of South Florida Library and Elaine Everly of the National Archives for their help with maps and manuscripts; and to Warren Anderson of the Winter Park office of the United States Geological Survey for sharing his expert knowledge of the St. Johns River.

Richard Le Conte Anderson of Macon, Georgia, has proved to be a valuable source of information about the Le Conte family, and I am also indebted to Mrs. C. H. McMillan of St. Simons Island, Georgia, for a picture of John Eatton Le Conte.

Professors Roland Browne and Jerrell Shofner, through their generous and patient suggestions, have put me on a firmer footing time and again, and my sister, Joanna Wallace, in typing the manuscript, has helped me to solve a score of editorial problems. I wish also to thank Jean Levy and Faith Umphrey for preparing the index.

My wife, Mildred, and my daughter, Jennifer, who trekked along the St. Johns with me from Puzzle Lake to Picolata, have helped most of all.

Introduction

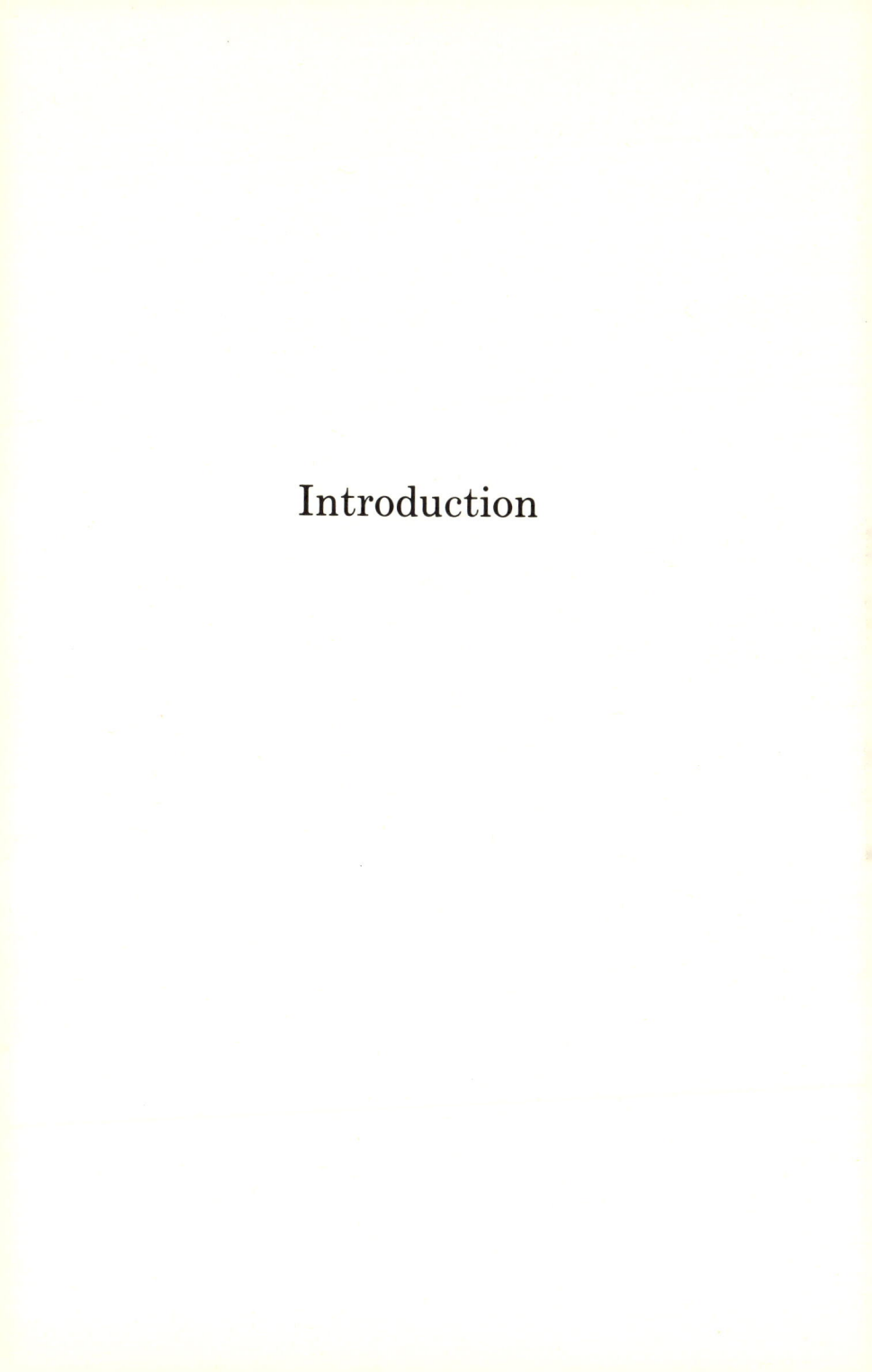

*How happily situated is this retired spot of earth!
What an elisium it is!*
WILLIAM BARTRAM, 1791

*After all, Florida is certainly the poorest country
that ever two people quarrelled for.*
JACOB R. MOTTE, 1838

AFTER nearly two and a half centuries, interrupted by twenty years of British possession from 1763 to 1783, the enfeebled Spanish rule of East Florida and West Florida ended in 1821. Although Americans had been settling in the Floridas for several years, not much was known about the interior of the larger, East Florida. The Spaniards had apparently left most of the interior untouched. Under the British there had been some noteworthy exploration and cartography, but these activities ended with the outbreak of the Revolution, and much of the topographical information they produced may not have been available to the United States government at the time of the 1821 cession.

Four men stand out among those who explored Florida between 1763 and 1776—the naturalists John and William Bartram and the cartographers William Gerard De Brahm and Bernard Romans. John Bartram (1699-1777) was already renowned as a botanist when he left his home in Philadelphia during the fall and winter of 1765-66 for a journey into coastal Georgia and up the St. Johns River in Florida, taking with him his son William (1739-1823). They journeyed as far as Salt Lake, about fifty miles from the source of the St. Johns, thinking that they had reached the source. "Billy," considered by his father aimless and likely to accomplish little, was later to become even more famous than John Bartram. In 1773, after two failures in business, he set out from his father's home to journey alone by boat, on horseback, and afoot through the Southeast. During his four-year odyssey, he would again travel up the St. Johns, almost as far as he had gone a decade earlier, and into the Indian nations of inland Florida. Bartram's *Travels* (1791), an unparalleled description of the unsettled Florida of the eighteenth century and a rich lode for modern naturalists, left its impression on the romantic movement in English literature.

Cartography in East Florida was concerned almost entirely with the coast. Louis De Vorsey, Jr., and P. Lee Phillips, among others, have described the undependable state of map making prior to 1770 and the attempts of William Gerard De Brahm and Bernard Romans to improve on it (11, 12, 44). De Brahm, surveying inland from the coast, had established by 1770 that Lake Okeechobee was not the source of the St. Johns (7, Plate V), but he put the source above Lake Harney, about where John Bar-

Introduction 5

tram had erroneously taken it to be. Even so, American map makers of the period do not appear to have known of his work.

In spite of the explorations of the Bartrams and of Romans and De Brahm, several questions remained unanswered: What was the interior lower half of the Florida peninsula like? Where was the true source of the St. Johns? Was there a feasible mode of water transportation through the territory from the Atlantic to the Gulf? How much arable land was there, and what crops and timber would grow? These questions and others like them, left in abeyance during the Revolution and the subsequent four decades of Spanish control, remained in 1821 for Americans to answer.

Questions of this sort, however, were secondary to other preoccupations: settlement and the claiming of land. Much of the activity of the new territorial government had to do with surveying and land claims, and less than fifteen years after the cession, war would erupt over government attempts to resettle the Seminole Indians. Thus it was not with federal officials that a proposal for the first United States exploration of East Florida originated. In April 1821, a few weeks after President Monroe announced the treaty giving the United States possession of the Floridas, John Eatton Le Conte, a thirty-seven-year-old captain in the Army Topographical Engineers, approached John C. Calhoun, then secretary of war, and proposed an expedition to explore Florida. Calhoun, doubtless preoccupied with political matters, suggested that Le Conte write to him later (21).

John Eatton Le Conte was well suited for the task of

exploring Florida. Born February 22, 1784, near Shrewsbury, New Jersey, the son of John Eatton Le Conte, Sr., and Jane Sloane Le Conte, he graduated from Columbia College and showed an early interest in science (56). In 1809, he wrote to one of his former professors at Columbia, Dr. David Hosack, to describe an epidemic of yellow fever in Georgia. His first botanical article, a catalogue of plants, appeared in 1811 in the *American Medical and Philosophical Register*, and from that time until the end of his life Le Conte published nearly forty articles on botany and zoology (56, pp. 12-16). Le Conte's talents also included drawing, and his color renderings of North American tortoises have merited him the cognomen "The Audubon of Turtles" (5). In fact, it was Le Conte who in 1840 first described and named the Florida terrapin, *Pseudemys floridana floridana* (15, p. 377).

The Le Conte name is distinguished in various scientific circles. John Eatton Le Conte's elder brother, Louis, born in 1782, inherited the family plantation, Woodmanston, near Midway in Liberty County, Georgia, and made it into a showplace of horticulture as well as a profitable rice plantation. John Eatton Le Conte, Jr., continued to live in the North but spent winters at Woodmanston. It was here in 1856 that he brought a pear tree that was later to be cultivated in Georgia as the Le Conte Pear (36; 49, pp. 67-68). Louis Le Conte's sons, John (1818-91) and Joseph (1823-1901), taught at Oglethorpe College, Franklin College, the University of Georgia, the University of South Carolina, and the University of California; and Joseph Le Conte's work in geology, biology, and philosophy earned him international recognition. John Eatton Le Conte's only son, the entomologist John Lawrence Le Conte (1825-83), accompanied

Introduction

Louis Agassiz on his explorations of the Great Lakes region and was the first man to navigate a considerable stretch of the Colorado River (40).

On April 13, 1818, John Eatton Le Conte was appointed captain in the United States Army Topographical Engineers. One of his first tasks was to survey the vicinity of Norfolk and to report on the geology of the surrounding countryside (10). Much of his work was apparently done in New York until early 1821, when he began to survey and chart the harbor of Savannah. On July 22, 1821, Le Conte was married in New York to Mary Ann Hampton Lawrence and was on furlough for several months thereafter (3, 10). During the following winter, he returned to the South and spent February and March 1822 exploring the St. Johns River.

Illness dogged Le Conte during the rest of his life, but he continued his scientific study and mapping. During much of 1823, he worked in Newark, New Jersey, and Portsmouth, New Hampshire, then returned to New York in 1824 to draw maps. Poor health, however, caused him to take a leave during July and August 1824 (10). In November 1824, he arrived with his wife in Savannah (53) and spent the following winter charting Ossabaw Sound, a task that he had laid aside when he went to Florida. By April 1825, the Le Contes were again in New York, where Captain Le Conte completed maps of the winter's work (10) and where his son, John Lawrence, was born on May 13 (3). The following November 19, on her way to the South, Mrs. Le Conte died (3). Captain Le Conte himself lay ill for six weeks in New York (10). During the remainder of his military service, Le Conte suffered from rheumatism and perhaps from other ailments. He spent the first half of 1826 recuperating in Georgia, probably at Woodmanston, and subsequent reports to the chief of engineers often cited the state of his health. Promoted to brevet major on April 18, 1828, "for 10 years faithful service in one grade," he continued to serve in the Topographical Engineers until August 20, 1831, when he resigned his commission. Le Conte never gave up his desire for exploration, however, and on February 13, 1845, he wrote to the chief of engineers asking permission to join an expedition to the Rocky Mountains, though apparently without success (10).

Major Le Conte continued to live at his old home at 46 Walker Street in New York at least until 1841, and Joseph Le Conte visited "dear old uncle Jack" there (34, p. 46). For the remainder of his life, Le Conte kept up his studies and his writing of scientific articles and was a fellow of the Linnaean Society of London as well as vice-president of the Lyceum of Natural History of New York. Later he moved to Philadelphia, where he was elected vice-president of the Academy of Natural Sciences. He died on November 21, 1860 (56).

Le Conte's idea for an exploration of Florida in 1821 was timely, but it hardly aroused much enthusiasm in the War Department. In fact, six months went by after his conversation with Calhoun before Le Conte himself revived the idea. After his marriage and subsequent furlough, Le Conte wrote to Calhoun on October 12, 1821, from his home in New York City, reminding the secretary of their conversation in April, informing him that he had been ordered to Georgia during the winter to continue surveying the Port of Savannah, and estimating that he would have four months to spend in Florida. He indicated that the expedition, which he expected not to cost over $1,000, was to have the following goals:

> First to investigate the quality of the soil determining the situation and quantity of the good land; that the government, when they come to dispose of may know in what manner to proceed in offering for sale, portions of a country which is almost entirely barren, in which at least the proportion of cultivable land is so small to that of pine barren.
> Secondly, to inspect the natural productions of the province, and by an examination of the climate, and the relative situation of different places, more accurately to determine the respective importance of each, both with regard to the value in a commercial and agricultural point of view: and to designate in a particular manner those sections of the country which produce timber fit for naval purposes, whether live oak, cedar, or mahogany, in order that the government may take proper steps for the preservation of an article daily becoming more scarce, and of course more costly. It is presumed that with regard to live oak some precautions on this head are highly necessary, as in a few years it will be impossible to obtain any more of that very necessary timber from Georgia. It is I believe calculated by those that are in the habit of cutting ship timber that from ten acres of live-oak forest scarcely two trees can be found from which timbers fit for the construction of the larger class of ships of war can be obtained. Lastly, to determine what means of communication can be formed between the Suwanney [sic] River and the St. John's, that the productions of the fertile country watered by the former river,

may be brought to a secure place of deposit, and thence transported to other parts of the union without the trouble and danger of a voyage round the Peninsula. To examine the possibility of forming a communication between Tampa Bay, Hillsborough River, and Lake George; that, if ever the first mentioned place be established as a naval depot, the necessary articles for such an establishment, furnished by the St. John's, may be brought to it with ease and with little expense: And finally to explore the St. John's river to its source, through a country utterly unknown, and it is believed as yet untrodden by the foot of a European (21).

Le Conte set forth the reasons that would appeal to a practical man like Calhoun: assessment of soil quality, the finding of ship timber, the charting of a short commercial route. Then, at the end, he gave his main reason for going: *to explore the St. John's river to its source, through a country utterly unknown, and it is believed as yet untrodden by the foot of a European.* For Le Conte, the essential thing was to know. The Florida expedition was worth undertaking for its own sake, apart from any economic benefits. To stress this, he ended his letter to Calhoun with the plea that, even if the first-named advantages were set aside, "at least the exploration of the river St. John's from its mouth to its source is worth the attention of government" (21).

Le Conte stressed exploration and discovery, and he was credited with the discovery of the source of the river by John Lee Williams and Charles Vignoles in the nineteenth century, as well as by Francis Harper, and by A. J. Hanna and James Branch Cabell in the twentieth. Le Conte obviously thought that his expedition had suc-

Introduction 11

ceeded in identifying the source—as John Bartram had thought half a century earlier—but several inadequacies and discrepancies indicate that he may have been mistaken. To begin with, he shortened the period of time for exploration, perhaps because of the indifference of army officials. In his October letter to Calhoun, Le Conte had estimated four months for the Florida expedition. Probably with a mind to using a government-owned vessel for several months in Florida, he wrote twice in October to Major General Alexander Macomb, chief of engineers, arguing that the army would save money by buying a sloop for him to use in surveying the Savannah harbor and the nearby Wassaw and Ossabaw sounds (22, 23). Evidently he was not authorized to buy the sloop, because on November 12, in Washington, he filed a requisition for the following funds for surveying the Georgia coast and the Florida interior:

Hire of a sloop for one month	$200
10 men for one month at $15	150
Subsistence for "	70
Signal poles, etc.	10
Case of mathematical instruments	36
Repairs	24
Contingencies	100
Exploring Florida	200
Extra pay	180
Total	$970

Le Conte had trimmed his time to one month, probably because rent for the sloop was so costly that it would be impossible for him to explore for three or four months and remain within his projected budget of $1,000. It is not clear why he asked for $200 for "exploring Florida" and another $180 for "extra pay." If it was all for himself, he was not to get any of it. Someone in the office of the chief of engineers crossed out the dollar amounts for the last three items and wrote "600" underneath Le Conte's total (24). This sum was sent to him. When he arrived in Savannah on December 3—the Savannah *Georgian* reported that three letters were being held in the post office for him on that day (51)—Le Conte wrote to General Macomb to acknowledge the receipt of the draft from the treasury and to express dissatisfaction "to find myself so much restricted in funds, as it will necessarily curtail the extent of my operations in this quarter" (25). In the same letter, he asked that orders be issued to military encampments in Florida to assist him and that "all the maps connected with E. Florida" be forwarded to him.

Le Conte at the time probably knew very little about Florida. No doubt he had read William Bartram's *Travels,* first published a quarter of a century earlier. Although John Bartram's journal was available as early as 1767 in a book by William Stork, Le Conte probably did not read it until near the end of his life, when he had access to the manuscript (6, p. 127). As for maps, the inaccuracy of American maps of this period compared to the one in which De Brahm had charted the source of the river suggests that Americans did not have access to De Brahm's map (7, Plate V). The British, after all, would not have handed over important maps to the United States government during the post-Revolutionary years. The 1822 map reproduced in this book (Map 2), a reproduction by Carey and Lea, is representative of the state of American map making in the early years of the century. It can be seen that Lake Mayaco (now Lake Okeechobee)

Introduction 13

was assumed to be the source of the St. Johns River. Le Conte, ascending the river with the same presupposition, was led into one of the most glaring errors in his report, that of denying the existence of any sizable lakes in the main channel above Lake George.

Besides being hampered by official indifference and poor maps, Le Conte may have become saddled with an unreliable exploring party. It was in late January or early February 1822 that he left Savannah for Fernandina to outfit his expedition. He arrived at Fernandina bearing a special order issued on February 1 by Major General Winfield Scott, commanding general of the Eastern Department, directing the commanding officer at Amelia Island to "furnish Capt. Le Conte eight men, and one non-commissioned officer armed & equipped for a command, say of six or ten weeks subsistence." The order went on to provide for "quarter masters stores & medicines," as well as for ordering soldiers to accompany Le Conte should the required number not volunteer (35).

At Fernandina, another officer joined the expedition, the only one of Le Conte's companions whose name is known. Lieutenant Edwin R. Alberti was a native of Pennsylvania who had left West Point after three years but had become an artillery officer without a degree from the academy. In the previous October he had been ordered from New York to St. Augustine to testify in a court-martial (60). When the trial ended he was ordered on January 18, 1822, to rejoin his company in the Second Artillery Regiment (35). "Exceedingly desirous to remain in the South" (2), he had managed within the next two weeks to attach himself to Le Conte's expedition and to have his place assured by his inclusion in General Scott's February 1 order. Later in the year, he was again to prove successful in remaining in the South. He secured a transfer to the Fourth Regiment, which was then stationed at St. Augustine. His record became intermittent after this, including sporadic periods of being absent without leave, and he was even for a time under arrest for refusing to obey an order to report to another post. Finally dropped from army rolls in 1827 after months of being absent from duty, Alberti resigned his commission shortly thereafter (47, 48). He settled in Florida, evidently prospering as a sawmill owner. In 1852, he wrote to the governor of Florida, asking to be excused from appointment to a receivership (1).

With Lieutenant Alberti, one noncommissioned officer, and eight enlisted men, Le Conte set out from Fernandina on February 10, 1822 (the day that he began recording daily temperatures); he passed through the Amelia Narrows (now Kingsley Creek) and then down the inland waterway to the St. Johns. On March 14, after thirty-three days, Le Conte recorded his last set of daily temperatures and probably reached Fernandina again on that day. By April 3, he was in Savannah, and from there he reported to General Macomb a summary of his expedition, promising to send a more detailed report later. During June, Le Conte was at West Point as a member of the Board of Visitors, supervising the annual examination (54), and during August and September he was forced by an outbreak of yellow fever to withdraw from New York to Newark to work on the report and a map of the St. Johns (10). On December 14, 1822, he finally wrote to General Macomb that he had completed the report on East Florida along with an accompanying map. He promised to deliver the report to Washington at the next meeting of the Board of Engineers (29). The map, however, cannot now be found.

Introduction

The Florida report, then, is only one of Le Conte's accomplishments, yet not one of his most satisfying, its value being vitiated by its sketchiness and frequent inaccuracy. If he kept notes, they must have been lost, and he had to rely too much on memory. One of the noted naturalists of his time, Le Conte mentioned virtually no Florida wildlife and very little of the native vegetation in his report. Yet one of his contemporaries reports that he came back from the expedition with many specimens (57, p. 23), and some of his finds would be the subjects of papers read in the later 1820s. Nor did he carry out his intended project of finding suitable ship timber. Given more time, he might have discovered Lake Okeechobee and explored the Oklawaha River and its valley. It is doubtful, however, that he could have done more than this. Without an extensive survey, he could not have fulfilled his intention of showing the feasibility of water transportation between the Atlantic and the Gulf.

Most disappointing, however, is Le Conte's inaccuracy. He concluded that the large lake rumored to be in the interior (Lake Okeechobee) did not exist, and he was skeptical about Florida's value. Worst of all, his description of the St. Johns above Lake George is simply wrong. Anybody ascending the river to its source would have to notice Lake Monroe and Lake Harney, yet Le Conte asserted that there were no lakes between Lake George and the source. This circumstance gives rise to the suspicion that he did not himself ascend to the headwaters of the St. Johns. It is probable that Le Conte, beset by illness near Lake George and interested in investigating the plant life in that vicinity, sent some of his men up the river to discover the source. The logical leader of such a detail would have been Lieutenant Alberti, who, in spite of having insisted on coming along, was not as interested in the outcome as Le Conte was. If Le Conte depended on others, they let him down. It would have been easy for them to row out of sight, then return several days later with a vague and inaccurate account patched together from guesswork and gleanings from Indians and white settlers.

In spite of these mistakes, Le Conte, aiming to set in perspective the extravagant claims made for Florida, was right about a number of things. He was right in his assessment of the impossibility of growing some crops, such as coffee, that had been mentioned for cultivation in Florida. He was right, also, about Tampa and Key West being better sites for fortifications than St. Augustine and Fernandina. Finally, he was right when he told of the great natural beauty of the unspoiled new territory.

Le Conte later contributed notably to knowledge about plant and animal life in America, but his Florida expedition of 1822, because of poor organization, the indifference of government officials, untrained personnel, and, regrettably, Le Conte's own shortcomings, resulted in a report that was insufficient and inaccurate. For all these reasons, Le Conte did not succeed in turning out a report that might have made his expedition the landmark that it ought to have been in the story of the exploration of Florida.

Observations on the Soil
and Climate of East Florida
John Le Conte, Captain, U.S. Army
February and March 1822

THE RIVER St. John's (called by the Indians Hîlaka,[1] or the river) in whatever point of view we consider it is one of the most remarkable objects in North America. That so large a body of water should arise in a perfectly level country and flow with the rapidity that this does (its mean velocity being three miles an hour)[2] is I believe a fact unexampled in the natural history of our globe. Its direction also from South to North, contrary to all other American rivers, is one of its most striking characteristics. These two circumstances have induced many writers to conclude that it is not a real river but an arm of the sea, and many are even now of opinion that its waters are salt from its mouth to its head, and that in some place its course is retrograde. In some old maps we see delineated rivers running from it into the Atlantic Ocean to the Southward of St. Augustine, in which case it would probably not be fresh, for the distance is so short, that the tide from the sea would without doubt flow into it; and this erroneous opinion of the water being salt has induced the constructors of these maps to form from their own imaginations rivers that never existed. But when we come to consider the configuration of the land in its neighborhood, the cause of its peculiar course and its great size will not be difficult to determine. Let us suppose the whole Peninsula to be one level plain of sand, through the midst of which a canal or waterway has been scooped out. Now if on one side of this and running parallel to it, there should exist a range of high hills, all the rain which falls upon them filtering through them, would naturally spring out at their bases, and if conducted to the great hollow which we have supposed to be made through the centre of the country, would go far towards filling it with water. The natural condition of the country perfectly agrees with this statement. On the Eastern side of the river, through almost its whole extent, and at no place more than half a mile from the edge of the water, the country consists of high pine land. On the western side from four to eight miles distance is an extensive range of sand hills, at least two hundred feet in height;[3] and on this side, there is as there ought to be from the position of these hills, more swamp than on the other, and generally reaching to the very base of the hills, except where the original surface of the earth has been sufficiently elevated to stand above the surface of the water, and has by the successive depositions of vegetable matter for a series of years become capable of supporting a vigorous vegetation and of resisting by its firmness the excessive rains of this subtropical climate. The level of this swamp is so little above that of the surface of the river, that what elevation it does possess seems scarcely more than what must arise from the protuberances of the roots of trees growing in it. It is always inundated; and being protected by the closeness of the growth from the united action of wind and sun, little evaporation ever takes place; and hence we may see the reason why in the driest season, scarcely any diminution in the quantity of water contained in the river is perceptible, for all that is carried off by the atmosphere, from the exposed surface, is immediately restored from those portions of its shores that are always under water.

It has as confidently been stated by some, as if they had been eye witnesses of the fact, that this river has its source in a large Lake called Mayaco, and on all our maps, a considerable portion of the interior is occupied by this extensive sheet of water.[4] There is, however, no such Lake in existence and its position on the maps has been owing to the misapprehension of the Spanish and English geographers. Its extreme source is a small lake about ten miles in circumference[5] that appears to have no name; in some old delineations of the inner parts of Florida, the river beyond Lake George is made to pass through three lakes of modest dimensions, but which of these is the one from which the river arises, cannot be determined, as there is nothing like any of them in its whole course, and it would be wrong to bestow upon a reality, the name that has been given to a fiction.[6] In a southernly and south easterly direction, as far as the eye can reach, extends a marsh or bay, overgrown with tall and coarse grass, differing in its nature from anything I have elsewhere seen, but most resembling those spots of low ground in the Southern states that are called pine barren ponds. The Seminole language, like that of all other barbarous nations, consists of but few words; only such as are necessary for the expression of their immediate wants, and refinement has not yet introduced among them those nice distinctions of terms that mark the language of polished nations; hence they have but one word to express what we discriminate by lake, pond, marsh, or bay.[7] Upon being asked where the St. John's had its source, they have answered in this immense marsh, and the word being translated Lake, has formed the Lake Mayaco, which I have ascertained by accurately questioning the natives has no existence. This marsh or bay may be considered as one great spring, continually pouring forth an abundant supply of water, and forms the chief source of this noble stream. It approaches according to very respectable authority very near to the sea, which at the head of the Lake is only eight or nine miles distant.[8] That the sea may once have occasionally communicated with the river by means of this marsh is not improbable, although now the water is perfectly fresh and contains as little saline matter as most streams. There is, however, one indication of a probable former communication with the sea: on the border of the Lake and particularly at its head, is found a great quantity of a species of grass which only grows in places that have been or now are subject to inundation by salt water.[9] After leaving the Lake, as the river is narrow, its course is crooked, and its width much diminished by various small branches, running out of it and afterwards coming in again, so as to form a kind of islands; all of these are destitute of any high land, and may have been formed posteriorly to the opposite shores; for in all parts of the river wherever the current happens to be diminished, there springs up an immense quantity of water lilies (vulgarly called water dock)[10] the roots and leaves of which matting together, intercept every thing that is brought down from above and in process of time so much earth is collected, that a sufficient support for small willows and other shrubs is afforded. The like causes continuing, and being increased by their own operation, may in the end collect a soil of sufficient quantity and firmness to support larger trees. I do not say that all the islands in the upper part of the river, and particularly the large ones have been thus formed, but the smaller ones certainly have, for the process is even now going on, and some of the lagoons are already so closed up as not to admit of a passage through them. The winding course of the river may be attributed to the nature of the ground through which it passes. On both sides with little interruption this is swamp or marsh; nothing therefore offered any resistance or restraint to the stream from following the course where its channel could be worn with the most ease, and thus it con-

Soil and Climate of East Florida

tinues until it enters Lake George, below which it is straighter and wider. It appears to have lately become a favourite theory with some that St. John's river has been formed by the junction of a number of lakes of different dimensions and has therefore been called a string of lakes. But it is not so; and although differing in some particulars from most other rivers, yet its form has nothing remarkable. Every river has bays and coves and is wider in some parts than in others, and yet it never has been said that all rivers are formed by the introversion of lakes. This certainly no more indicates such a formation, than the Hudson, the Ohio, or the Mississippi. That its water may once have overflowed a great portion of the neighboring country, and that it is now diminished in width cannot be doubted; for the same Helices and other little shells that now inhabit at the bottom of the river, are found deposited in incredible quantities everywhere on its shore. The same appearance indeed of a diminished quantity of water may be observed in every lake and river; in every one we can find traces of their present shores. But whether this diminution has been gradual or instantaneous, is I conceive impossible to determine: it seems in all places where like appearances are observed, that the water has retreated at different periods, and with long intervals between, but every day's experience teaches us that these changes must have occurred long before the existence of any historical records, and that things have remained on the surface of our earth pretty much in the same state as they now are for an almost indefinite period.

Lake George, the entrance to which from either side is rendered difficult by shoals to vessels of any size, possesses a mean depth of twelve feet: it is fourteen or fifteen miles long and six or eight wide. As we enter from below, its appearance is grand and imposing; and owing to the lowness of the land, the trees of its farthest extremity are scarcely visible even when the atmosphere is most transparent and the view the least obstructed. Besides the water of the river flowing into this large basin, there are on the west side two sources or fountains that afford an immense supply, probably more than the river itself.[11] These fountains are of a very peculiar nature: there are others like them farther up the river, but not so large, nor so deserving notice. But before we proceed to the description of these two, it may be well to mention the others, particularly their situation and respective differences. In all the water is perfectly transparent, and of a bluish cast, and more or less impregnated with mineral substances: the most distant one[12] is on the edge of the lake at the head of the river and is strongly impregnated with sulphur and some bitter salt, its temperature 70°; the next[13] is some distance lower down and contains an equal quantity of sulphur but less saline matter, its temperature 75°; a little above the head of Lake George is a third,[14] without any sulphurous taste or smell and containing but a small quantity of other foreign matters, temperature 65°. Below Lake George also there is a fourth[15] sulphurous Spring whose temperature does not vary from that of the river. The head of Long Lake,[16] which is a kind of river running into the St. John's from the East and distant [nine] miles from it, is a fountain of the same nature, but rather lower in its temperature than any of the others.[17]

Nearly midway between the mouth of Lake George and its head in proceeding along the western shore, we suddenly perceive an entire change in the colour of the water, which from being black and opaque becomes all at once perfectly transparent. A current of considerable force issues from a small creek;[18] following this up to its source, we find its origin to be an immense fountain at least twenty yards in diameter, near the center of which is a continual ebullition, the water being thrown up about a foot from the level of the basin. It is so extremely diaphanous as to appear as if no medium of greater density than the atmosphere was intended between the eye and the bottom, which in some places is four or five fathoms deep. The smallest objects lying on the ground at this depth are as distinctly perceptible as if suspended in the air before us:[19] different kinds of fish may be distinguished by their shape and colour more accurately than if viewed at an equal distance out of the water. There must be several tons of water discharged from this spring every minute,[20] and the quantity and violence of its discharge is said never to diminish. Whence, there is a natural question, does this proceed? and where are we to look for the cause of so remarkable an appearance? The country on the back of the spring is a range of lofty hills that bound an extensive Savannah everywhere interspersed with lakes. Should this Savannah be proved to be higher than the immediate shores of the river, the problem will be easily solved.[21] Nor is it any objection that the Aklowâhâ, which rises in the same savannah is a sluggish stream; for the difference in the rapidity of two rivers that rise in the same place and at an equal altitude, and discharge themselves at other places which are likewise of the same level although at a distance from each other, will be in the inverse ratio of the length of their respective courses. But to account for the saline impregnation in the case before us is not so easy; it is probably mercuriate of lime[22] that gives the bitter and unpleasant taste to this water, but it never could receive this except from the decomposition of some minerals existing beneath the surface. Observation, as far as it can be intended, affords us no proof that this can be so. All the stony matter that exists anywhere in Florida is a loose and recently formed aggregation of sea shells, or a hard and flinty rock analogous to flint or petrosilex, which exists in immense quantity in the Alâchuâ country, and evidently at some remote period must itself have been nothing but a mass of shells; from neither of these by any known opinion of natural causes would this salt be extracted. The peculiar transparency of this water, to which the reflection of the sky above and the white sand beneath give a bluish tinge, is another remarkable circumstance, which cannot but strike the attention of every beholder. The cause of the different colours of many waters never can be satisfactorily explained; it is a problem in Opticks perhaps impossible to solve.[23] In all large bodies of this fluid, the reflected light which gives us the idea of the colour always comes from strata below the surface, and therefore when we attempt to reason from experiments made upon small quantities of water we invariably fail in a true result. It will be observed also that the light reflected from any fluid is very different from that which is transmitted through it, when there is any quantity acted upon. It has been said that when there is no absorption of rays, the transmitted light must be the complement of the reflected; granting this to be so, what change can be produced in two bodies of the same nature, that will cause one to absorb so much of a given quantity of light, as to prevent it from reflecting the remainder as it ought, and in the other to absorb none? When taken up in a glass vessel the water of the lake is as transparent as that of the spring, but the former when in a mass, as has been observed before, is nearly black. I am aware that alcohol and some solutions of neutral salts are much more transparent than most other liquids; but no knowledge of the laws of light and vision can teach us how this happens.

One of the most remarkable things in this fountain is the immense quantity of fish that inhabits it. It is incredible how many are to be seen sporting about in every direction; no comparison can give any definite idea of their number, and they all move about in perfect safety, careless of everything around, none appearing to have the least apprehension even of those that are their natural enemies, the most ravenous passing in perfect calmness those that in other situations are their daily prey. Some of these are species that only inhabit on the borders of the ocean, to wit, the skate and stingray.[24] How they ever got here and have become accustomed to live in fresh water is inexplicable, unless we suppose that the sea in former ages had a communication with the river. The banks of this fountain and of the creek that issues from it are much higher land than any immediately adjoining. On the southern side is one entire grove of oranges, and the remainder of the growth consists of such trees as tend by their beauty or by the fragrance of their flowers, to give a peculiar charm to the forests of a warm climate. In these delightful solitudes where winter has no power, nature never ceases to appear in her most attractive garb, and flourishes in unfading beauty throughout the year. Yet this spot, so capable of exciting in every thinking mind those pleasing sensations which we feel when wandering through the vast and primeval solitudes which the presence of man has rarely interrupted, must hereafter be invaded and contaminated by him. The forests that now wave with such majesty around will be levelled to the earth, and every vestige of those beauties which at present are able to attract the notice of even the most illiterate and unfeeling, vanish before the destructive influence of human cupidity.

The salt spring[25] (as it is called) is situated a few miles lower down the Lake, and is of the same nature as the one which we have just described. There is no perceptible ebullition in its basin, and the creek which issues from it, having to run nearly five miles before it reaches the lake, becomes discoloured and muddy. It is very salty at its mouth; although the water at the fountain does not indicate a greater proportion of saline impregnation than the great spring, its temperature like that of the other is 78°. This fountain is nearly seventy yards in diameter; it rises directly at the foot of the hills before mentioned, and it is not more than half a mile to a part of the great Savannah which occupies so much of the West of the river. The head of a large and long lake[26] approaches also to the very base of these hills on the other side, and consequently makes the ridge in this part very narrow, giving it the appearance of a high and narrow embankment. The Savannah with this lake winding through it extended as far as the eye could reach although viewed from an eminence two hundred feet above it.[27]

Did this river run through a fertile country, its value to the inhabitants would be incalculable, for excepting the shoals at its entrance, and the bars at the mouth and head of Lake George, it admits of a perfectly free navigation for vessels of above a hundred tons burthen, to within thirty yards of its termination. It may hereafter be made use of to form an internal communication between the gulf of Mexico and the Atlantic ocean, and thus free the intercourse between all our maritime States and Louisiana from the danger and expense of a voyage round Cape Sable.[28] Where this canal shall be formed, and from what waters on the Western shore of the Peninsula it shall be directed, remain hereafter to be determined, from a minute examination of the intervening country, and a due consideration of the benefits that will result from each different point of junction.

Upon entering the river by the inland passage from St. Mary's,[29] the first object that strikes the view is the very unusual circumstance of a hilly country. All the eastern side at this point is undulating; and the hills are not solitary and insulated, but consist of a regular and uninterrupted chain, such as occurs in submountainous countries. The soil here on both sides of the river is superior in quality to any that is afterwards met with: on the western side indeed it is bordered by an extensive marsh which renders it difficult to approach, but at different intervals small creeks enter it from the river and generally head in the high land. The growth has been chiefly live oaks, in some places mixed with pine: the first have long ago disappeared, and can only now be recognized as having once existed there, by the indestructible quality of their remains which no exposure can destroy in much less than a century. St. John's bluff,[30] where there once was a fort and probably a town, if the Spanish accounts of the former flourishing state of the province can be relied on, is a very high and commanding position, well situated to guard the entrance of the river and prohibit all approach by sea. The undulating land before mentioned, continues nearly as far up as Julianton creek,[31] but gradually loses its character near that point, until it sinks into the monotonous uniformity of the low country of all the Southern states. It, however, does not yet assume that unvaried aspect of sterility and utter uselessness, that belongs to almost all the country on the St. John's. The Western side is not as good as the Eastern and on neither side is there any pure pine barren. Advancing farther up the river, the soil gradually deteriorates, small patches of good land being found at long intervals. At the mouth of McGirth's creek,[32] however, there appears to be a considerable body of what in other situations would be deemed valuable land, as there is a thick growth of live oak upon it; but whether this tree in Florida is an indication of fertility as it is in Georgia, may be questioned, for the want of any severe cold in winter, or the assemblage of many peculiarities of climate with whose operations we are unacquainted may produce here the same effect that real fertility of soil does in other countries, or vice versa. In Georgia where what is strictly called live-oak land chiefly occurs, it is of two kinds: that of the interior which consists of blue clay covered to some depth with vegetable mould and which is inexhaustible, and that of the coast and of the sea islands, where the soil is sand, mixed with oyster shells, and thinly coated with a similar mould; this, although at first very productive in almost anything that is cultivated in it, must in the end become exhausted and useless. The live-oak land of Florida is of a quality different from both these and I should think, drawing my conclusions from what is observable in other countries, far inferior; it more nearly resembles what in Georgia is called Laurel land, a solid sand mixed near the surface with very black mould and superimposed on yellowish clay. We do not by any means consider this as the first quality, for it soon wears out and becomes incapable of producing anything; but, as I observed before, nothing really conclusive can be drawn from this comparison, so great are the differences produced by climate. What in the Southern states is reckoned our best land, in the Latitude of 40° N. would be of no value and conversely, for all countries may be considered as being constituted in such a manner as to be best suited to their own natural productions, or to such as can be assimilated to them, and in the first settlement of every country, the primary operations of men, must necessarily be nothing more than experiments.

It is this lower part of the river alone that is settled, for some miles farther up indeed are a few habitations and vestiges of many more that have long been deserted, sad monuments of the folly and visionary extravagance of the English when in possession of this country. At Picolata[33] the Spaniards and the English in their time kept a garrison which was strengthened and supported by a fortification on the West side, but both these have long ago fallen to decay, and of the last nothing is now remaining. They were undoubtedly constructed to keep the Indians in awe and to protect the inhabitants, especially such as were situated below. They must have essentially answered this purpose and it is therefore somewhat surprising that the Spaniards, on their occupation of the province at the close of the revolutionary war, should have deserted them and then left the whole country open to the incursions of the Seminoles, then a powerful nation.

From a little above this point, the orange tree may be said first to appear as indigenous;[34] groves of different sizes are every where interspersed in the woods, and invariably indicate

Soil and Climate of East Florida

land of a very light and poor quality. At a point below Buena Vista[35] is the first large grove, and the contemporaneous growth of the forest, is such as never occupies a rich soil, namely laurel and pine. Here also we begin to see the commencement of those swamps of considerable depth, which afterwards are so common, but so situated as to be incapable of being rendered productive: indeed could they be drained or employed for the cultivation of rice, it is very questionable whether it would be worth the trouble to attempt it, for they promise no reward to the labour that must then be bestowed upon them. Instead of the noble and lofty cypresses and large Tupelos which are produced by land of this nature in other parts of our country, we see here chiefly maples and water oaks, and these small, although bearing marks of extreme age. Amidst all the swamp that skirts the borders of the river, there are points of high land, hills as it were rising out of the level sand of the surrounding country, and these spots of high land constitute all the visible portions of soil that ever can be cultivated. They are found in small and detached parcels from five to twenty acres and separated from each other by extensive tracts of Pine barren and swamp. In all other rivers of the Southern states the points of land are invariably covered with pine, but in this with a growth of another kind; this is a peculiarity in which this river differs from all others in America. The Pine barrens, which constitute the chief part of the province and may be considered as occupying the whole of the interior, but rarely approach the river nearer than a quarter of a mile; and when they do form the bank, it is not for any very great extent. This it would be said arises from the river having once been wider than it is at present, whence all the low land may be considered as having once formed the bed of the river. But when this was the case, if ever, is not apparent; neither can it explain the reason of all the projecting points being covered with vegetable mould to some depth, when the rest of the high land in the immediate vicinity is not so, but consists of barren white sand. If we except Black creek[36] and the Oklâwâhâ river, there are no streams of any consequence tributary to the St. John's; all the others are mere drains of internal swamps. And even the outlet of Dunns Lake is little more.[37] This interesting feature in the Topography of the country I can only speak of from information derived from others, as I was prevented from personally examining it. It is a large body of water about [twelve] miles long and [three] broad. If we cut off the indentations of its coves, it would form a perfect oblong rectangle. Its outlet is about nine miles in length, nearly straight and enters the river by three distinct mouths. There are also three streams running into it from the East, all of which arise very near the sea, and may even at times when an easterly wind raises the tides above their usual altitude communicate with it, for it is said that at times the water of one of them is so salt that horses will not drink of it. The land on its bank resembles that of the river, and is of no value for agricultural purposes.

With regard to the probable cultivation of valuable articles in this country, I cannot but consider all the recent speculations on the subject as visionary. The possibility of raising coffee, and thus supplying the consumption of this necessary article of diet from among ourselves, has been seriously contended for.[38] The highest expectations of profit have been raised by supposing that a new application of labour could be made, and the false reports of designing and unprincipled men have been brought forward to prove that the soil of Florida particularly on the sea coast was admirably adapted to it. But if we consider that there is probably no plant more impatient of cold than the coffee and that even under the tropics in elevated land and in exposed situations, a cold wind frequently prevents it from perfecting its seeds, how can we expect it to flourish in a country every part of which is liable to severe frosts. Sugar undoubtedly will thrive here better than in Louisiana, but there is very little land capable of producing it.[39] Unless a body of such soil sufficient to employ the capital and the labouring force of local men can be obtained, they certainly cannot be induced to remove from their own settlements to a new country and it is not from the poor and solitary emigrants that we can expect the establishment of plantations every way expensive and insecure.

Rice is exclusively calculated to occupy low ground which otherwise would remain untilled. There are in the province immense tracts of swamp, but none of it is fertile, and little capable of being drained. The want of rich high land, which will prevent the introduction of the sugar cane, will also act as an impediment to the cultivation of Cotton. These comprise every thing that a country like this can be supposed able to produce, with a hope of remuneration for labour. The Olive tree may succeed, but it remains to be proved how far it can be made productive, either with regard to its oil or its preserved berries; and in what manner the attention of the inhabitants can be drawn toward an object, which at best holds forth a distant and a yet precarious source of revenue.[40] I pass over the idle visions of some writers respecting articles of less importance and by one example shall endeavour to shew how futile they are. The Date Tree, which in countries incapable of producing better articles of food is considered so valuable and indeed is indispensable to the preservation of life, has been mentioned as peculiarly worthy of attention. There is no doubt that this tree will thrive equally as well in Florida as it does in the South of Europe; but those who please themselves with the idea of its ever being of more value in America than any other saccharine fruit of either warm or cold climates will be entirely mistaken. In no point of view can it be compared to the fig; it is slower of growth and its product is much less: the fig, on the other hand, in a short time and without any trouble arrives at maturity, yet who ever heard of this fruit being dried and prepared for exportation in any part of North America? Both this and the dates have been known from the remotest settlement of the province to flourish everywhere in it, and yet both are rare.[41] There is in the inhabitants of Florida as well as in those of our southern states an indolence of disposition; that prevents them from taking advantage of the peculiar qualities of their climate, if unconnected with immediate and extensive profit; hence in no part of the world is fruit, except such as is indigenous, so scarce and of such bad quality as in these countries and it is rarely that we meet with anyone who has attempted to introduce from other places any vegetables that might be naturalised among them. Florida has always been over valued; it therefore becomes our duty to lay aside the expectations of an El Dorado or a fountain of immortality, and by a diligent scrutiny, by practical experiments, and the application of a labour that no difficulty can interrupt, nor disappointment daunt, strive to discover the best uses to which our newly acquired territory can be applied.[42]

The climate of the interior can be best judged of from the annexed table of thermometrical observations.[43] I shall therefore merely observe that during the whole of the time when I was there, no frost was visible; indeed at the head of the river, there had been none, for autumnal plants were there in full bloom, and mixed with the flowers of early spring. The air was soft and agreeable; when the wind blew from the Southward, the horizon had the same appearance, as is observed in the more southern States during that indeterminate portion of autumn called the Indian Summer. The great quantity of lofty palm trees, and the parasitic plants with which they are sometimes covered, together with a species of fern which sometimes attains to the height of seven or eight feet,[44] give to parts of the country the features of a West Indian landscape. The whole extent of the river, according to the reports of Indians and other inhabitants, is extremely unhealthy; and but little difference in this respect is observable between the summer and winter. A different state of things cannot be expected, when we find the process of vegetable putrefaction going on without interruption during every season of the year. In those parts of the river where the surface is covered with the floating plants of the Pistia (vulgarly called water lettuce)[45] the air appears to be particularly pestiferous and its ill effects upon the constitution remain long after we are removed from its immediate influence.

It only remains for me to make some observations relative to the military posts in the province. There are at present but two, Fernandina on Amelia Island[46] and St. Augustine.[47] The first is entirely useless, and should be immediately abandoned. As for the second, it may be well always to occupy it, and in time of war to maintain a strong garrison in it; for the folly of our enemies will certainly lead them to overlook points of more importance and to attack this. Although in reality an object of no importance to an enemy, and not worth the expense of time and men necessary for its reduction, yet their being in the occupation of it, might cause some trouble and interrupt the peace and comfort of our southern states. If however my opinion relative to the establishment of new posts be asked, I should decidedly say that it was necessary to establish at least one company at Tampa bay,[48] and another somewhere near the point of the peninsula,[49] to prevent any smuggling and the illegal introduction of slaves into the country as well as to destroy the horde of pirates, privateers and wreckers, who make their chief rendezvous somewhere near these points. In time of war these two positions may be of much value to ourselves, and thus a double effect be produced: the banishment of a numerous horde of banditti from our territories; and the occupancy of two posts that in such a case may be extremely serviceable to us.

John Le Conte, Captain
U.S.: Top. Engr.

STATE OF THE THERMOMETER IN EAST FLORIDA DURING THE MONTHS OF FEBRY AND MARCH 1822

			Sunrise	3 o'clock	Sunset	
Febry	10	rain	30	38	32	}
	11	clear	29	36	32	} In Amelia Narrows
	12	"	35	64	58	
	13	"	44	74	60	
	14	hazy	49	67	64	
	15	clear	54	76	69	
	16	"	54	76	72	
	17	rain	65	75	73	
	18	clear	66	78	69	
	19	"	58	70	66	
	20	cloudy	62	74	72	
	21	clear	73	88	84	in the Sun 105
	22	cloudy	71	70	64	
	23	rain	54	75	65	
	24	cloudy	52	77	71	
	25	"	50	61	61	
	26	"	50	72	67	
	27	clear	54	70	71	
	28	"	60	75	73	in the Sun 105
March	1	cloudy	58	77	78	
	2	foggy	66	88	84	
	3	rain	77	79	75	
	4	cloudy	44	55	58	
	5	"	52	76	64	
	6	"	48	73	70	
	7	"	54	71	64	
	8	rain	62	83	73	
	9	rain	54	64	56	
	10	rain	52	58	54	violent storm from NE
	11	"	48	51	49	storm continues
	12	clear	56	70	72	
	13	"	54	82	76	
	14	"	60	86	78	

Notes

1. William A. Read, basing his information on Daniel G. Brinton's *Notes on the Floridian Peninsula* (Philadelphia: J. Sabin, 1859), p. 154, and on William Darby's *Memoir on the Geography . . . of Florida* (Philadelphia: T. E. Palmer, 1821), p. 85, says: "The Seminoles called the St. Johns River *Ylaco* or *Walaka*. *Ylacco* seems to be intended for Creek *wi-lako*, 'river,' or 'big water,' whereas *walaka* is a corruption of Creek *wi-*, or *wiwa*, 'water,' and *alaka*, 'coming'— hence 'tide,' 'intermittent spring' " (45, p. 39).

2. At its normal stage, the St. Johns River drops twenty-four feet from its headwaters to its mouth, not nearly enough to move with this exaggerated velocity.

3. About eight miles west of Lake George lies a range of hills that rise as high as 180 feet above sea level.

4. Bernard Romans wrote in 1775 that a Spanish pilot had told him about having been taken to Lake Mayaco (Lake Okeechobee) when he had been captured by Indians. Romans thought that "it is not improbable" that the St. Johns flowed from the lake (50, p. 285). American map makers, following Romans' supposition, showed Lake Mayaco as the source until the 1820s, when most apparently began to agree with Le Conte's description of the source (see Selected List of Maps). John Cary's New Map of Part of the United States of North America (1806) (Map 1) exemplifies this error, as does the Carey and

Lea Geographical, Statistical, and Historical Map of Florida (1822) (Map 2). Henry Schenck Tanner's Map of Florida (1823) separates "Lake Macaco" from the river and shows the source of the river south of "Monroe's Lake," suggesting that Tanner may have known of Le Conte's report (see Map 3).

John Lee Williams concluded that there was not enough evidence to show that the lake existed (66, p. 61). He noted that de Soto had encountered near Tampa Bay an Indian chief named "Macaco" and inferred that the name "Mayaco" simply alluded to the domain of this chief. As late as 1828, he talked with Indians who referred to the Charlotte River as "Macaco" yet knew nothing of a large lake in the interior. As a result, he left the lake off his 1837 map of Florida.

Le Conte, on discovering that the large lake was not the source, failed to hypothesize that the geographical features exist separately but instead asserted that the lake did not exist. This conclusion caused Williams to repeat the same error fifteen years later. Although subsequent map makers would show the lake, it was not until 1886 that an expedition would penetrate the dense vegetation around the lake and accurately map Lake Okeechobee (16).

5. The actual source of the river may have been discovered long before Le Conte's expedition, but its whereabouts were apparently not known to American map makers. There is a claim in Moll's Atlas (1720) that a Captain T. Nairn of South Carolina, with a raiding party of Yamassee Indians, ascended to the source of the St. Johns in 1706. This atlas, however, is far from accurate. More probable is the claim by William Hayne Simmons that about 1780 Andrew Turnbull, a kinsman and namesake of the founder of the New Smyrna Colony, traveled overland around the head of the river (57, p. 24).

Two of his contemporaries credited Le Conte with finding the source of the St. Johns. Simmons wrote that Le Conte had found it "about fifty miles beyond Lake George" (57, p. 24), but this location does not correspond to Le Conte's figures, as it places the source in the vicinity of Lake Monroe. Charles Vignoles reported that Le Conte had found the source "at the identical head lake" that John Bartram had reached in 1766 (64, pp. 66–67), i.e., Salt Lake. A century later James Branch Cabell and A. J. Hanna, quoting from Le Conte's report, credited him with the discovery of the source (8, p. 264).

The St. Johns River originates in a marsh about thirty miles northeast of Lake Okeechobee. Blue Cypress Lake, or Lake Wilmington, in the middle of the marsh, is about three hundred miles from the mouth of the river and is about ten miles in circumference. However, Mr. Warren Anderson of the United States Geological Survey has pointed out to me that there is no discernible channel between Blue Cypress Lake and Lake Helen Blazes to the north. In the thirty-three days that Le Conte was navigating the river, he could hardly have gone beyond Lake Helen Blazes, if he got that far. Yet he describes the source in two other places. On April 8, 1822, he wrote in a preliminary report: "This river . . . takes its rise in a small lake about ten miles in circumference, nearly three hundred miles from its mouth. Beyond this lake extends a marsh as far as the eye can reach, and bounds the sight with as level and uninterrupted horizon as the sea itself. This marsh is constantly under water, and therefore may be considered as one great spring (or spring bog, as such places are more emphatically named by the inhabitants of the Southern States) from which water is slowly but continually oozing out, and which is not materially affected in its appearance by dry or wet seasons" (27). Le Conte again described the source on August 21, 1826, when he read a scientific paper to the Lyceum of Natural History of New York:

> In the spring of the year 1822, whilst engaged in exploring the river St. John, on the borders of the small lake which forms the source of that stream, I could perceive no effects of the winter: autumnal plants, such as different species of Eupatorium and of Aster, were in full bloom at the same time with Violets and Irides, which are peculiarly vernal. A season thus lengthened out by the absence of cold, of course allows many plants to grow in perfection, which a shorter duration of warm weather would not permit to exist.
> The extensive savannahs, the boundless swamps, and the ancient forests, as yet unpolluted by the encroachments of men, present a variety of objects equally new and interesting. The long fronds of the Acrostichum aureum, frequently eight feet in height, the pendent Isaria, and towering Palms, and the parasitic plants which clothe the branches and trunks of many of the trees, all impress upon the mind the assurance of our having entered a country differing essentially in many things from the temperate regions of the more northern states (33, p. 129)

Between these two descriptions the verbal picture of a spring bog shades into that of groves of palms and other trees, suggesting some kind of confusion in Le Conte's mind about the appearance of the headwaters.

6. Nothing in Le Conte's report casts more doubt on its author's credibility than this astonishing statement. It is conceivable that Le Conte thought of Lake Monroe and Lake Harney, both "lakes of modest dimensions," as mere widenings in the river. In his preliminary report, however, he stated that the river varies "in width from fifty to two hundred yards" between its source and Lake George (27, p. 1). Lake Monroe is three miles wide and Lake Harney two miles across.

7. The name *Mayaco* is probably of the same origin as *Miami*. "Writing in 1575 Fontanedo mentions a lake by the name of *Mayaimi*, which he translates as 'very large.' This name, of which *Miami* is a variant, may be a compound of Choctaw *maiha*, 'wide,' and *mih*, 'it is so.' By *Laguna de Mayaimi* Fontanedo meant what is now called *Lake Okeechobee*. Avilés, on his expedition up the St. Johns River in 1566, called this lake *Maymi*" (45, p. 18). (It should be added that Pedro Menéndez de Avilés did not reach the lake, being turned back by Indians above Lake George.) Indian place names that suggest a lake generally use the Seminole-Creek word *wiwa*, "water" (45, pp. 40–41 and passim). Thus Le Conte's etymology is wrong.

8. Le Conte's saying that he had this information "on very respectable authority" establishes that the statement was not based on direct observation. This distance from the sea would apply either to the marsh east of Blue Cypress Lake or to Salt Lake, southeast of Lake Harney, which John Bartram had erroneously taken to be the source of the river.

9. Le Conte's imprecision leaves a lot of room for guesswork. He must have found here a grass that he had seen before, perhaps *Spartina*, some species of which grow along the east coast in brackish marshes.

10. The yellow water lily (*Nuphar luteum*) is referred to as spatterdock, not water dock. The name water dock is applied now to *Rumex verticillatus*, or sheep sorrel, by Robert W. Long and Olga Lakela in *A Flora of Tropical Florida* (Coral Gables: University of Miami Press, 1971), pp. 410, 376. Taxonomies vary from botanist to botanist, however, with common names showing more durability than Latin names.

11. Silver Glen Springs and Salt Springs (see notes 18–25).

12. This is probably Juniper Creek, which enters the lake near the south end.

13. According to Richard Mills, ranger at the Juniper Springs Recreation Area in the Ocala National Forest, numerous springs bubble from shell mounds along the river. Even with his help, I have been unable to identify either this spring or the "fourth," which Le Conte says is "below Lake George."

14. Probably Blue Creek, which is not spring fed and hence would have a lower temperature in winter. The springs in this vicinity do not have temperatures below 70°.

15. See note 13.

16. Lake Dexter.

17. Ponce De Leon Springs, or Spring Garden Lake, flows into Lake Woodruff, which is connected to Lake Dexter. Le Conte left a blank before "miles."

18. The creek flowing from Silver Glen Springs is only half a mile in length.

19. In his preliminary report, Le Conte wrote: "There are fountains of the most perfectly limpid water bursting with violence from the bowels of the earth and pouring out uninterrupted and unfailing streams. So transparent is the water of these springs and with such force do they issue from their subterranean reservoirs, that they run to a considerable distance without mingling with the black water of the river; and an approach to one of them is immediately perceived by the sudden and entire change of colour in the surrounding element. In these places which are generally pretty deep, the smallest object may be perceived at the bottom. At the great spring, or silver spring as some call it, which is on the border of Lake George, the man who ascertaining the depth, through carelessness suffered the sounding line to slip out of his hand, yet at the depth of six fathoms, there was no interruption of vision resulting from much water even in a state of agitation, but the line was distinctly perceived, and without much difficulty regained by means of a fishing line. Were I minutely to describe this place or others of a similar character, both time and materials would fail me, and what is worse I should exhaust your patience. I shall therefore only observe concerning all the waters of these large springs, that they have a mineral impregnation which renders them unfit for use, some of sulphur and all of salt; their temperature varies from 75° to 80°" (27). Those who claim medicinal

properties for Salt Springs and Silver Glen Springs might quarrel with Le Conte's evaluation of the water in these springs.

20. On April 24, 1956, during a dry year, 108 cubic feet per second poured from Silver Glen Springs, or about 210 tons per minute (62).

21. Hopkins Prairie, northwest of Silver Glen Springs, is about thirty feet above sea level, whereas the spring itself is at sea level.

22. The Central Florida Crime Laboratory has confirmed that the water of Silver Glen Springs does indeed contain mercuriate of lime.

23. According to a physicist with whom I discussed this passage, the darker color of lake water is owing to the presence of algae and tannic acid and to dark sediment on the bottom rather than to an optical phenomenon.

In the following year, on December 1, 1823, Le Conte delivered a paper in which he further affirmed his faith in the impenetrability of nature. "How apt are we to suffer ourselves, in our researches, to be drawn aside from certainty and truth by a foolish desire of accounting for every thing! Nature is covered with a thick veil, which cannot be penetrated: a proud spirit and an ambitious presumption may lead us to suppose that we have been enabled to remove the covering which she throws over her operations, but every day's experience shows us the absurdity of publishing our vague hypotheses for established truth, and the still greater absurdity of attempting to defend them" (19, p. 54).

24. Rays and other saltwater fish are still sometimes seen in Lake George, having entered the St. Johns from the ocean. No doubt in 1822 some of these fish were present in the springs along the lake.

25. John Livingston Lowes, in *The Road to Xanadu,* showed how William Bartram's description of Salt Springs entered Samuel Taylor Coleridge's subconscious mind and reemerged in "Kubla Khan." Bartram wrote: "Just under my feet was the inchanting and amazing crystal fountain, which incessantly threw up, from dark, rocky caverns below, tons of water every minute, forming a bason, capacious enough for large shallops to ride in, and a creek of four or five feet depth of water, and near twenty yards over, which meanders six miles through green meadows, pouring its limpid waters into the great Lake George, where they seem to remain pure and unmixed. About twenty yards from the upper edge of the bason, and directly

Notes 47

opposite to the mouth or outlet to the creek, is a continual and amazing ebullition, where the waters are thrown up in such abundance and amazing force, as to jet and swell up two or three feet above the common surface: white sand and small particles of shells are thrown up with the waters, near to the top, when they diverge from the center, subside with the expanding flood, and gently sink again, forming a large rim or funnel round about the aperture or mouth of the fountain, which is a vast perforation through a bed of rocks, the ragged points of which are projected out on every side" (15, pp. 165-66).

In 1797, Coleridge, after mixing his Bartram with his opium, slept, dreamed, then woke up to write:

> And from this chasm, with ceaseless turmoil seething,
> As if this earth in fast thick pants were breathing,
> A mighty fountain momently was forced;
> Amid whose swift, half-intermitted burst
> Huge fragments vaulted like rebounding hail,
> Or chaffy grain beneath the thresher's flail:
> And 'mid these dancing rocks at once and ever
> It flung up momently the sacred river.
> Five miles meandering with a mazy motion
> Through wood and dale the sacred river ran,
> Then reached the caverns measureless to man,
> And sank in tumult to a lifeless ocean.

26. Lake Kerr and Little Lake Kerr.

27. Le Conte must mean two hundred feet from the east shore of Little Lake Kerr, rather than two hundred feet in elevation. He viewed the lake from the ridge between the lake and Salt Springs.

28. The notion of a cross-Florida canal is one of the most persistent in United States history. Le Conte treats it as though it was a familiar idea in his day.

29. Kingsley Creek, then known as the Amelia Narrows.

30. The 1560s had seen two bloody battles at St. Johns Bluff. In 1562, the French established Fort Caroline there, but its Huguenot defenders were killed or driven away in 1564 by the Spaniards, who renamed it Fort San Mateo. In 1567, the French retaliated with an attack on the Spanish occupants. There was indeed a town established at St. Johns Bluff about 1779 by British loyalists. Named Johns

Town, it was abandoned in 1783 when Britain ceded the Floridas to Spain (8, pp. 123-27).

31. Julington Creek.
32. Ortega River. The name of McGirth's Creek is a memorial to Dan McGirth, a notorious outlaw whose dramatic life ended in imprisonment and madness (8, pp. 128-32).
33. There are no longer any traces of the forts at Picolata, on the east bank, and Fort Poppa, on the opposite shore. The site was at the crossing of the Old Spanish Trail from St. Augustine to Pensacola, and the forts were probably built about 1700 out of coquina rock. Bartram describes Fort Picolata as follows:

> This fortress is very ancient, and was built by the Spaniards. It is a square tower, thirty feet high, invested with a high wall, without bastions, about breast high, pierced with loop holes and surrounded with a deep ditch. The upper story is open on each side, with battlements, supporting a cupola or roof; these battlements were formerly mounted with eight four-pounders, two on each side.
> The works are constructed with hewn stone, cemented with lime. The stone was cut out of quarries, on St. Anastatious Island, opposite St. Augustine: it is of a pale reddish brick colour, and a testacious composition, consisting of small fragments of sea shells and fine sand. It is well adapted to the constructing of fortifications. It lies in horizontal masses in the quarry, and constitutes the foundation of that island. The castle at St. Augustine, and most of the buildings of the town, are of this stone (15, p. 80).

According to one contemporary of Le Conte, nothing remained of Fort Picolata in 1822 but two broken walls pierced with loop holes (64, p. 67).

34. "There are . . . very small Groves consisting of nothing else than sour and bitter-sweet Orange Trees. These latter Groves have been planted by the Spanish horse Party, scouting from Saint Augustine, which always carried a Provision of those Oranges with them, and planted the Seeds wherever they halted to refresh or encamped. These Orange Trees sprouted, grew to Trees, bore Fruit in three or four years time, and increased themselves from the dropping Oranges

which rotted on the Ground, became Dung to the Seeds, and were covered by the Winds with Earth" (12, p. 213). Mrs. W. P. Carter of Oviedo has told me that early planters in the Oviedo area went to the coast in the 1870s to bring back trees for use as root stock.

35. Buena Vista, shown on present-day maps as Dancy Point, is on the east bank below Palatka.

36. Black Creek flows into the river south of Doctors Inlet.

37. Crescent Lake. I have included the dimensions of the lake where Le Conte unaccountably left blank spaces.

38. William Darby points out that coffee can be grown successfully only where the temperature remains above 65° F. for many consecutive months and that at St. Augustine (latitude 29° N) in January 1766 ice stood an inch thick (9, p. 32). Another contemporary, William Hayne Simmons, also notes that "it is now known, that in the course of every two or three years, the influence of frost is felt as far down as the Cape of Florida, and often on the keys beyond. This circumstance totally precludes the cultivation of coffee, as this plant is not merely nipt, but entirely killed by the slightest frosts" (57, p. 25).

39. As early as 1766 Richard Oswald had established a sugar plantation near what is now Ormond Beach. It was bought by Charles W. Bulow in 1821 and renamed Bulow Ville. A number of sugarcane plantations, with mills, flourished on the east coast during the 1820s and 1830s, only to be destroyed by Indians during the Second Seminole War. Today extensive sugar cultivation is carried on farther south. A. J. Hanna and Kathryn Abbey Hanna have discussed the Florida sugar plantations in *Florida's Golden Sands* (Indianapolis: Bobbs Merrill, 1950).

40. Although olives frequently grow where oranges grow, the successful cultivation of olives requires temperatures above 59°–60° F. (9, pp. 30–31).

41. Date cultivation, which needs temperatures 75° F. or above, may be possible in parts of Florida, but figs can be raised at temperatures as low as 62° F. (9, p. 34).

42. Le Conte's first impression of Florida was little different from this jaundiced evaluation: "Those large bodies of rich and valuable land that we have been taught to expect here, are no where to be found. Add to this an unhealthy climate, and an atmosphere that infects the inhabitants with fever, as well in the summer as the winter,

and I think that the assertion of this never becoming a populous country is well founded and that insurmountable obstacles are opposed to its ever becoming of such value as it was supposed it would. It is in vain to point out a beautiful river, with the advantage of an excellent navigation; when it cannot be brought to minister to the use or cupidity of man; it will always be avoided, in as much as the evils always attendant upon low grounds and water courses are not compensated by fertile and productive ground" (27). Doubtless Le Conte felt that he needed to counter propaganda like the following, printed by the land developer Denys Rolle in 1766: "Every thing in nature seems to correspond towards the cultivation of the productions of the whole world, in some part or other of this happy province, the most precious jewel of his majesty's American dominions" (quoted in 42, p. 51).

43. Although it is impossible to guess where Le Conte was when he recorded most of his temperature readings, it appears that he visited Florida during an exceptionally mild winter.

44. *Acrostichum aureum* (see note 5).

45. "The former masses of water lettuce (*Pistia stratiotes*) on the St. John's have been largely replaced by water hyacinth (*Eichhornia crassipes*) introduced from the tropics about 1884" (15, p. 352). Willie Lee Sieg, of Geneva, has told me that early settlers used to eat the water lettuce.

46. Fort San Carlos on Amelia Island was built about 1816 and abandoned "soon after 1821" (59, pp. 19, 31). Apparently the Amelia Island garrison was still using the fort in March 1822, when Le Conte was last there.

47. Castillo de San Marcos at St. Augustine was begun by the Spanish in 1672 and completed in 1696 (38).

48. Less than a year after Le Conte's expedition, on March 5, 1823, a party under the command of Lieutenant Colonel George M. Brooke began clearing a site on Tampa Bay for a fort later to be known as Fort Brooke (39, p. 133).

49. Even before Le Conte finished his report, Lieutenant William H. Allen of the schooner *Alligator* was killed on November 8, 1822, fighting pirates, who sailed freely in the Gulf of Mexico and Florida Bay (63, p. 147). Soon thereafter, on February 1, 1823, Commodore David Porter commanded a force that began to establish a naval base and marines barracks at Key West (63, p. 148).

Notes 51

Le Conte may not have been quite fair in classing wreckers with pirates. About forty to fifty wreckers, based at Nassau, used Key Tavernier as a rendezvous, and their main threat to the United States consisted in their bringing an annual revenue of £15,000 to the British government. They often performed useful services by piloting ships out of dangerous waters, and they were sometimes the dupes of unscrupulous ship captains who sailed away without paying for their aid (64, pp. 125-27).

Bibliography

1. Alberti, E. R. Letter to Thomas Brown, Governor of Florida, 9 January 1852. Library of Florida History, University of Florida.
2. Alberti, Edward R. Letter to the Adjutant General, U.S. Army, 23 June 1822. Letters Received by the Adjutant General. Microfilm 567, roll 1, no. 21, National Archives, Washington.
3. Anderson, Richard Le Conte. Letter to Richard Adicks, 13 October 1975.
4. Anderson, Warren, and D. A. Goolsby. *Flow and Chemical Characteristics of the St. Johns River at Jacksonville, Florida*. State of Florida Department of Natural Resources Information Circular no. 82. Tallahassee, 1973.
5. "The Audubon of Turtles." *Georgia Alumni Record* 51 (March 1972):15–18.
6. Bartram, John. *Diary of a Journey Through the Carolinas, Georgia, and Florida from July 1, 1765, to April*

10, 1766. Annotated by Francis Harper. Philadelphia: The American Philosophical Society, 1942.
7. Bartram, William. *Travels in Georgia and Florida, 1773-1774.* Annotated by Francis Harper. Philadelphia: The American Philosophical Society, 1943.
8. Cabell, James Branch, and A. J. Hanna. *The St. Johns: A Parade of Diversities.* New York: Farrar and Rinehart, 1943.
9. Darby, William. *A Memoir on the Geography and Natural and Civil History of Florida.* Philadelphia: T. E. Palmer, 1821.
10. DeGrange Index. Records of the Corps of Engineers. Record Group 77, National Archives, Washington.
11. De Vorsey, Louis, Jr. "De Brahm's East Florida on the Eve of Revolution: The Materials for Its Recreation." In *Eighteenth-Century Florida and Its Borderlands,* edited by Samuel Proctor. Gainesville: The University Presses of Florida, 1975.
12. De Vorsey, Louis, Jr., *De Brahm's Report of the General Survey in the Southern District of North America.* Columbia: University of South Carolina Press, 1971.
13. Fairbanks, George R. *History of Florida.* Philadelphia: J. B. Lippincott, 1871.
14. Forbes, James Grant. *Sketches, Historical and Topographical of the Floridas*; *more particularly of East Florida.* 1821. Edited by James W. Covington. Floridiana Facsimile and Reprint Series. Gainesville: University of Florida Press, 1964.
15. Harper, Francis, ed. *The Travels of William Bartram,* Naturalist's Edition. New Haven: Yale University Press, 1958.
16. Heilprin, Angelo. *Explorations on the West Coast*

of Florida and in the Okeechobee Wilderness. Philadelphia: Wagner Free Institute of Science, 1887.
17. Heitman, Francis R. *Historical Register of the United States Army from . . . 1789 to . . . 1903.* Vol. 1. Washington: U.S. Government Printing Office, 1903.
18. *A History of the LeConte Family and the Woodmanston Plantation.* Savannah, Georgia: The Georgia Conservancy, 1975.
19. Le Conte, John Eatton. "Description of a New Species of Siren, with Some Observations on Animals of a Similar Nature." *Annals of the Lyceum of Natural History of New York* 1 (1824):52-58.
20. Le Conte, John Eatton. "Description of a New Species of Siren." *Annals of the Lyceum of Natural History of New York* 2 (1828):133-38.
21. Le Conte, John Eatton. Letter to John C. Calhoun, 12 October 1821. Microfilm 221, roll 93, National Archives, Washington.
22-30. Le Conte, John Eatton. Letters to General Alexander Macomb, in Letters Received by the Chief of Engineers. Record Group 77, National Archives, Washington. (22) 12 October 1821; (23) 23 October 1821; (24) 12 November 1821; (25) 3 December 1821; (26) 3 April 1822; (27) 8 April 1822; (28) 23 June 1822; (29) 14 December 1822; (30) 16 May 1824.
31. Le Conte, John Eatton. "Observations on the North American Species of the Genus Gratiola." *Annals of the Lyceum of Natural History of New York* 1 (1824):103-8.
32. Le Conte, John Eatton. "Observations on the Soil and Climate of East Florida, February and March 1822." Record Group 77, National Archives, Washington.

33. Le Conte, John Eatton. "On the North American Plants of the Genus Tillandsia, with Descriptions of Three New Species." *Annals of the Lyceum of Natural History of New York* 2 (1828):129-32.
34. Le Conte, Joseph. *The Autobiography of Joseph Le Conte.* Edited by William Dallam Armes. New York: Appleton and Company, 1903.
35. Letters Sent by the Eastern Division of the U.S. Army, Records of U.S. Army Continental Commands, 1821-1920. Record Group 393, National Archives, Washington.
36. *The Louis Le Conte Botanical and Floral Garden.* Hinesville, Georgia: Liberty County Historical Society, [n.d.].
37. Lowery, Woodbury. *The Spanish Settlements within the Present Limits of the United States.* 1. *1513-1561.* 2. *Florida, 1562-1574.* New York: G. P. Putnam's Sons, 1911.
38. Manucy, Albert C. *The Building of Castillo de San Marcos.* National Park Service Popular Study Series: History, no. 16. Washington: U.S. Government Printing Office, 1945.
39. McCall, George A. *Letters from the Frontiers.* 1868. Edited by John K. Mahon. Floridiana Facsimile Series. Gainesville: University of Florida Press, 1974.
40. *The Men of the Time, or Sketches of Living Notables.* Clingon Hall, N.Y.: Redfield, 1852.
41. Morris, Allen. *Florida Place Names.* Coral Gables: University of Miami Press, 1974.
42. Mowat, Charles L. *East Florida as a British Province, 1763-1783.* New Haven: Yale University Press, 1943.

43. Myers, Robert Manson. *The Children of Pride: A True Story of Georgia and the Civil War.* New Haven: Yale University Press, 1972.
44. Phillips, P. Lee. *Notes on the Life and Works of Bernard Romans.* DeLand, Florida: The Florida State Historical Society, 1924.
45. Read, William A. *Florida Place-Names of Indian Origin and Seminole Personal Names.* Baton Rouge: Louisiana State University Press, 1934.
46. Register of Letters Received by the Secretary of War. Microcopy 22, National Archives, Washington.
47. Returns from the Fourth Regiment of Artillery, July 1822 to July 1827. (Returns from Regular Army Artillery Regiments, June 1821 to 1901.) Microcopy 727, roll 25, National Archives, Washington.
48. Returns of the Second Regiment of Artillery, October 1821 to June 1822. (Returns from Regular Army Artillery Regiments, June 1821 to 1901.) Microcopy 727, roll 9, National Archives, Washington.
49. Rogers, William Warren. *Thomas County, 1865–1900.* Tallahassee: Florida State University Press, 1973.
50. Romans, Bernard. *A Concise Natural History of East and West Florida.* New York, 1775.
51. Savannah *Georgian,* 3 December 1821, p. 3, col. 1.
52. Savannah *Georgian,* 30 July 1822, p. 3, col. 1.
53. Savannah *Georgian,* 22 November 1824, p. 2, col. 4.
54. Savannah *Museum,* 18 June 1822, p. 3, col. 2.
55. Savannah *Republican,* 2 December 1825, p. 2, col. 4.
56. [Sharswood, William.] "John Eatton Le Conte: a Necrology." *Pamphlets on Collective Biography,* vol. 7, no. 3 (1860).
57. Simmons, William Hayne. *Notices of East Florida.*

1822. Edited by George E. Buker. Floridiana Facsimile Series. Gainesville: University of Florida Press, 1973.
58. Simpson, J. Clarence. *Florida Place-Names of Indian Derivation.* Edited by Mark F. Boyd. Florida State Board of Conservation Special Publication no. 1. Tallahassee, 1956.
59. Smith, Hale G., and Ripley P. Bullen. *Fort San Carlos.* Notes in Anthropology, vol. 14. Tallahassee: Florida State University, 1971.
60. Special Order no. 16. Orders Issued by the Eastern Department, U.S. Army, p. 218. National Archives, Washington.
61. Stork, William. *A Description of East Florida, with a Journal Kept by John Bartram.* London: W. Nicoll, 1769.
62. *Surface Water Supply of the United States: Part 2-B.* South Atlantic Slope and Eastern Gulf of Mexico Basin, Ogeechee River, and Pearl River. Geological Survey Water-Supply Paper 1434. Washington: U.S. Government Printing Office, 1958.
63. Tebeau, Charlton W. *A History of Florida.* Coral Gables: University of Miami Press, 1971.
64. Vignoles, Charles. *Observations Upon the Floridas.* New York: E. Bliss and E. White, 1823.
65. Wheat, James Clement, and Christian F. Brun. *Maps and Charts Published in America Before 1800*: *A Bibliography.* New Haven: Yale University Press, 1969.
66. Williams, John Lee. *The Territory of Florida.* New York: A. T. Goodrich, 1837.

Selected List of Maps

1720 H. Moll, New Map of the North Parts of America Claimed by France. Florida Historical Society Collection, University of South Florida.

This map notes that Captain T. Nairn of South Carolina ascended to the source of the St. Johns in 1706.

1722 Carte du Mexique et de la Floride. Florida Historical Society Collection, University of South Florida, no. 50.

This map shows a large lake, called "Serrope," about where Lake Okeechobee should be.

1770 Wm. Gerard De Brahm. Map of the General Surveys of East Florida, Performed from the year, 1766 to 1770. (From Crown Collection of Photographs of American Maps, ser. 1, vol. 5, no. 49,

1907.) Reprinted in William Bartram, *Travels in Georgia and Florida, 1773-1774*. Annotated by Francis Harper. (Philadelphia: The American Philosophical Society, 1943), Plate V.

De Brahm shows the "head of St. Juan's Stream" west of Cape Canaveral, about where John Bartram supposed it to be.

1806 John Cary. A New Map of Part of the United States of North America. Florida State University Library (see Map 1 in this volume).

1810 R. F. Tardieu and P. J. Valet. Carte de la Flor-
(?) ide et de la Georgie. P. K. Yonge Library of Florida History, University of Florida, no. 758.

This is unique in showing a town named Mayaco in the vicinity of Lake George.

1816 John Melish. Southern Section of the United States. P. K. Yonge Library of Florida History, University of Florida, no. 226.

Melish is typical of map makers of the period, showing the St. Johns as flowing from Lake Mayaco.

1821 William Darby and B. Tanner. Florida. Florida Historical Society Collection, University of South Florida, no. 86.

This map shows the source of the St. Johns as "South Lake," which is north of a marsh called "Lagoona Mayax."

Selected List of Maps

1822 Geographical, Statistical, and Historical Map of Florida. Carey and Lea Atlas, no. 37. Philadelphia. Florida Historical Society Collection, University of South Florida (see Map 2 in this volume).

1824 Henry Schenck Tanner, Map of Florida. Philadelphia. Florida Historical Society Collection, University of South Florida, no. 33 (see Map 3 in this volume).

1824-26(?) Map of Florida According to the Latest Authorities. Florida State University Library.

This map shows the source of the St. Johns as being close to "Lake Mayaca."

1837 John Lee Williams. Map of Florida. New York. Florida State University Library.

Williams leaves Lake Okeechobee off his map.

1838 T. G. Bradford. Florida. Florida Historical Society Collection, University of South Florida, no. 44.

This appears to be the earliest map to use the name "Lake Okeechobee."

Maps

Map 1

A detail from John Cary, A New Map of Part of the United States of North America (1806). (Courtesy, Florida State University Library.)

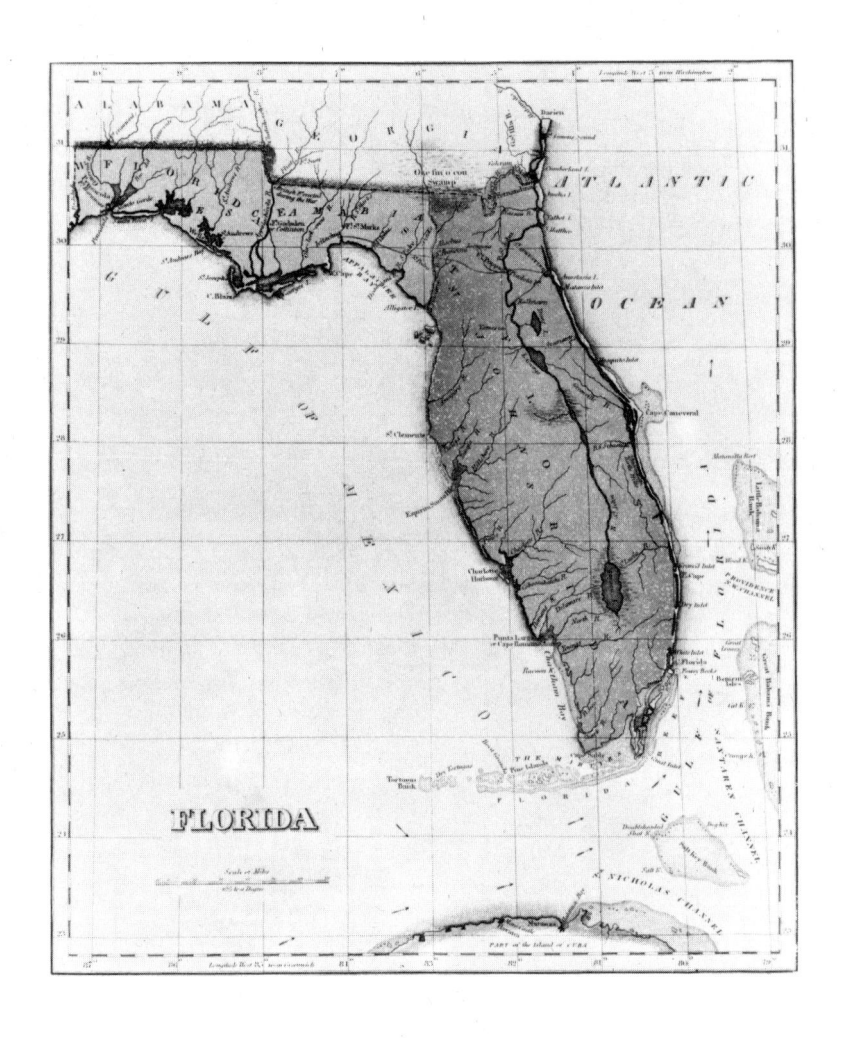

Map 2

Geographical, Statistical, and Historical Map of Florida,
Carey and Lea Atlas, no. 37(1822).

Map 3

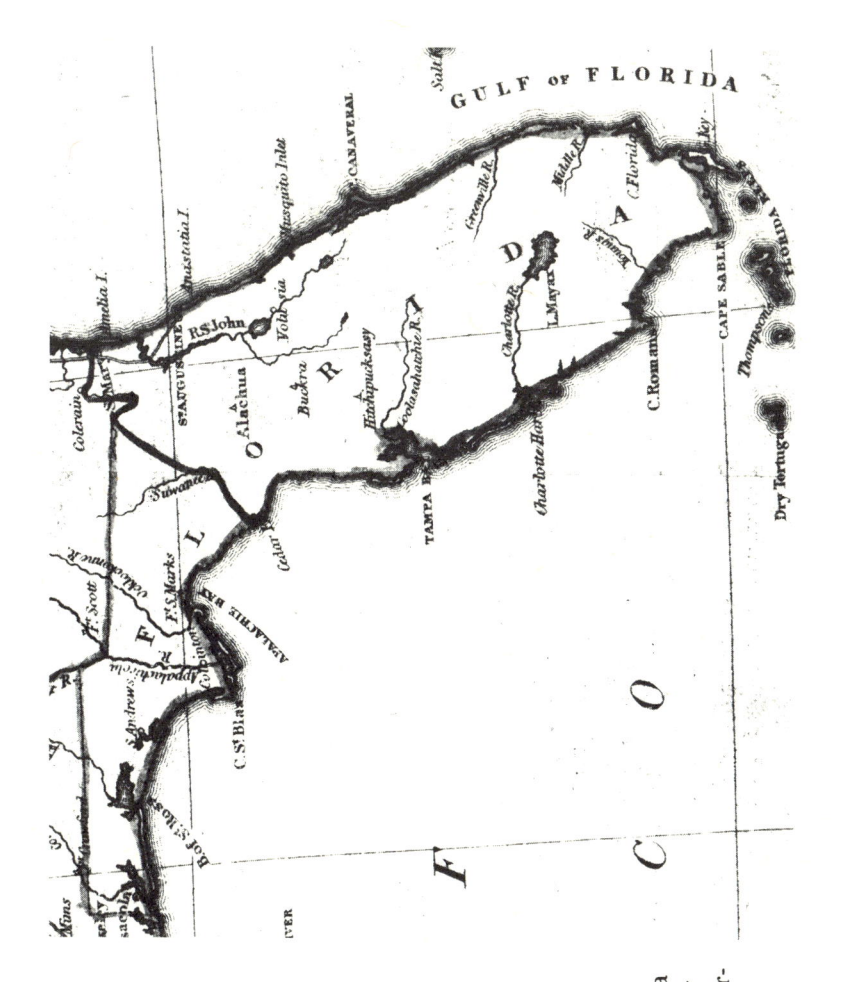

Henry Schenck Tanner, Map of Florida (1824?). (Courtesy, Florida Historical Society Collection, University of South Florida.)

Index

Academy of Natural Sciences, Philadelphia, 8
Acrostichum aureum, 43, 50
Agassiz, Louis, 6
Aklowâhâ, 25. *See also* Oklawaha
Alachua country, 25
Alberti, Edwin R., lieutenant, 13, 14, 16
Allen, William H., lieutenant, 50
Alligator, U.S.S., 50
Amelia Island, Florida, 13, 35, 50
Amelia Narrows. *See* Kingsley Creek
American Medical and Philosophical Register, 6
Anderson, Warren, U.S. Geological Survey, 43
Aster, 43
Atlantic Ocean, 5, 15, 28

Audubon, John James, 16
"Audubon of Turtles, The." *See* Le Conte, John Eatton, major
Avilés, Menéndez de. *See* Menéndez de Avilés, Pedro

Bartram, John, 4, 11, 12, 42, 44
Bartram, William: *Travels* (1791), 4; quoted, 3, 48; mentioned, 12, 16, 46
Black Creek, 32, 49
Blue Creek, 45
Blue Cypress Lake (Lake Wilmington), 42, 43, 44
Board of Engineers, 14
Board of Visitors, West Point, 14
Brooke, George M., lieutenant colonel, 50
Brooke, Fort, 50
Brown, Thomas, governor of Florida, 14
Buena Vista, 31, 49

INDEX

Bulow, Charles W., 49
Bulow Ville, 49

Cabell, James Branch, 10, 42
Calhoun, John C., secretary of war, 5, 8, 10
California, University of, 6
Carey and Lea's Atlas, 12
Caroline, Fort, 47
Carter, Mrs. W. P., 49
Castillo de San Marcos, 51
Central Florida Crime Laboratory, 46
Charlotte River, 42
Choctaw language, 44
Climate of Florida, 49–50
Coffee, suitability as crop, 16, 32, 49
Coleridge, Samuel Taylor, 46
Colorado River, 7
Columbia College, 6
Coquina, 48
Cotton, 33
Crescent Lake, 49
Cross-Florida Canal, 28, 47
Cypresses, 31

Dancy Point, 49. *See also* Buena Vista
Darby, William, 49
Date cultivation, 33, 49
De Brahm, William Gerard, 4, 12
De Soto, Hernando. *See* Soto, Hernando de
De Vorsey, Louis, Jr., 4
Dexter, Lake, 45
Doctors Inlet, 49
Dunns Lake, 32. *See also* Crescent Lake

Eastern Department, U.S. Army, 13
East Florida, 3, 12, 14
Eichhornia crassipes. See Water hyacinth
Eupatorium, 43

Fern, 35
Fernandina: starting point of expedition, 14; mentioned, 13, 16, 35
Figs, 34, 49
Flint, 25
Flora of Tropical Florida, A. See Long, Robert W.
Florida, Cape of, 49
Florida Bay, 50
Florida's Golden Sands, 49
Fontanedo, Hernando, 44
Fountains: on Lake George, 24. *See also* Salt Springs; Silver Glen Springs
Fourth Artillery Regiment, 14
Franklin College, 6
Frost, prevalence of, 34, 49

Geneva, Florida, 50
George, Lake: dimensions and depth of, 23; sulphur springs near, 24; sandbars, 28; limit of Avilés expedition, 44; saltwater fish in, 46; mentioned, 10, 13, 15, 21–28 passim, 41–42. *See also* Silver Glen Springs
Georgian, Savannah, 12
Great Lakes, 6

Hanna, A. J., 10, 42, 50
Hanna, Kathryn Abbey, 50

Index

Harney, Lake, 4, 15, 44
Harper, Francis, 10
Helen Blazes, Lake, 43
Helices, 23
Hîlaka (St. Johns River), 19
Hillsborough River, 10
Hopkins Prairie, 46
Hosack, David, M.D., 6
Hudson River, 23
Huguenots, 47

Indians, 44
Irides, 43
Isaria, 43

Johns Town (St. Johns Bluff), 47-48
Julianton Creek. *See* Julington Creek
Julington Creek, 29, 48
Juniper Creek, 45
Juniper Springs Recreation Area, 45

Kerr, Lake, 47
Kerr, Little Lake, 47
Key Tavernier, Florida, 51
Key West, Florida, 16, 50
Kingsley Creek, 14, 37, 47
"Kubla Khan," quoted, 46

Laguna de Mayaimi. *See* Miami
Lakela, Olga, 44
Laurel land, 30
Le Conte, Jane Sloane, 6
Le Conte, John (1818-91), 6
Le Conte, John Eatton, major: proposes exploration of St. Johns, 5; early years, 6; publications, 6; "The Audubon of Turtles," 6; and Le Conte pear, 6; joined Topographical Engineers, 7; resigned from army, 8; letter to J. C. Calhoun, 8; report assessed, 15; evaluation of Florida, 49-50; mentioned, 10, 11, 12, 14
Le Conte, John Eatton, Sr. (father of Major John Eatton Le Conte), 6
Le Conte, John Lawrence (1825-83), 6, 7
Le Conte, Joseph (1823-1901), 6, 8
Le Conte, Louis (b. 1792), 6
Le Conte, Mary Ann Hampton Lawrence, 7
Le Conte pear, 6
Liberty County, Georgia, 6
Linnaean Society of London, 8
Live-oak trees, 9, 28
Long, Robert W., 44
Long Lake, 24. *See also* Dexter, Lake
Louisiana, 28, 33
Lowes, John Livingston, 46
Lyceum of Natural History of New York, 8, 43

Macaco, 42
Macaco, Lake, 38. *See also* Okeechobee, Lake
McGirth, Dan, 48
McGirth's Creek, 29, 48
Macomb, Alexander, major general, chief of engineers, 11, 12, 14
Maples, 31
Mayaco, 42, 44. *See also* Okeechobee, Lake
Mayaimi. *See* Miami

Index

Maymi, 44
Menéndez de Avilés, Pedro, 44
Mercuriate of lime, 25
Mexico, Gulf of, 5, 15, 28, 50
Miami (variant of Mayaimi), 44
Midway, Georgia, 6
Military posts, 35
Mills, Richard, U.S. Forest Service, 45
Mississippi River, 23
Moll's Atlas (1720), 42
Monroe, James, President, 5
Monroe, Lake, 15, 42, 44
Monroe's Lake. *See* Monroe, Lake
Motte, Jacob R., quoted, 3

Nairn, T., captain, 42
Nassau, Bahama Islands, 51
Newark, New Jersey, 7, 14
New Smyrna, Florida, 42
New York City, 7, 14
Norfolk, Virginia, 7
Nuphar luteum. See Water lilies

Ocala National Forest, 45
Oglethorpe College, 6
Ohio River, 23
Okeechobee, Lake: not source of St. Johns, 4; called Lake Macaco or Mayaco, 12; Le Conte doubted existence of, 15; early knowledge of, 41–42; first charting of, 42; called Laguna de Mayaimi, 44
Oklawaha River, 15, 25, 32
Old Spanish Trail, 48
Olives, 49; tree, 33
Optics, 26
Orange groves, 27; trees, 30, 48

Ormond Beach, 49
Ortega River, 48
Ossabaw Sound, Georgia, 7, 11
Oswald, Richard, 49
Oviedo, Florida, 49

Palatka, Florida, 49
Palm trees, 34, 43
Pensacola, Florida, 48
Petrosilex, 25
Philadelphia, 4, 8
Phillips, P. Lee, 4
Picolata, 30, 48
Pine barren, 31
Pine trees, 28
Pirates, 35
Pistia. See Water lettuce
Ponce De Leon Springs, 45
Poppa, Fort, 48
Porter, David, commander, U.S. Navy, 50
Portsmouth, New Hampshire, 7
Privateers, 35
Pseudemys floridana floridana. See Terrapin, Florida

Rays, 46
Rice, 33
Road to Xanadu, The, 47
Rocky Mountains, 8
Rolle, Denys, 50
Romans, Bernard, 4, 41
Rumex verticillatus. See Sheep sorrel

Sable, Cape, 28
St. Augustine, Florida: Lt. Alberti on assignment here, 14; site of fort, 16, 35; terminus of Spanish Trail, 48; mentioned, 19, 49, 51

Index

St. John's Bluff, 29, 47, 48
St. John's River: explored by John and William Bartram, 4; as link to interior of Florida, 9; Lake Okeechobee thought to be source of, 12–13, 21, 41; Le Conte begins exploration of, 14; Le Conte mistaken in description of, 15; called Hílaka, 19; theory of formation, 23; tributaries, 32; "unhealthy" climate, 35; true source of, 42–43; Avilés expedition, 44; saltwater fish in, 46; water hyacinths, 50; mentioned, 5, 7, 10, 19–32 passim
St. Mary's River, 28
Salt Lake, 4, 42, 44
Salt Springs, 24, 27, 44, 46, 47
San Carlos, Fort, 50
San Mateo, Fort, *See* Caroline, Fort
Savannah, Georgia, 7, 13, 14; port of, 8, 11
Scott, Winfield, major general, 13
Second Artillery Regiment, 13
Second Seminole War, 49
Seminole-Creek language, 42
Seminole Indians, 5, 41
Seminole language, 21, 44
Sheep sorrel (*Rumex verticillatus*), 44
Shrewsbury, New Jersey, 6
Sieg, Willie Lee, 50
Silver Glen Springs, 24, 44, 45, 46
Simmons, William Hayne, 42, 49
Skate, 26
Slaves, illegal trade in, 35

Soil quality, 28, 29, 31
Soto, Hernando de, 42
South Carolina, University of, 6
Spanish Trail, 48
Spartina, 44
Spring Garden Lake (Ponce De Leon Springs), 45
Stingray, 26
Stork, William, 12
Sugarcane, 33; plantations, 49
Sulphur, 24
Suwannee River, 9
Swampland, 31

Tampa, Florida, 16
Tampa Bay, 10, 35, 42, 50
Tanner, Henry Schenck, 42
Temperatures: of water, 24; table of, 37; of springs, 45
Terrapin, Florida, 6
Timber for shipbuilding, 9
Topographical Engineers, U.S. Army, 7, 8
Tortoises, North American, 6
Tupelos, 31
Turnbull, Andrew, 42

United States Geological Survey, 43

Vignoles, Charles, 10, 42
Violets, 43

Walaka, 41
War department, U.S., 8
Washington, D.C., 11, 14
Wassaw Sound, Georgia, 11
Water dock, 22, 44
Water hyacinth (*Eichhornia crassipes*), 50

Water lettuce (*Pistia*), 35, 50
Water lilies, 22; yellow (*Nuphar luteum*), 44
Water oak, 31
West Point, 13, 14
Williams, John Lee, 10, 42
Wilmington, Lake. *See* Blue Cypress Lake
Woodmanston, Liberty County, Georgia, 6, 7
Woodruff, Lake, 45
Wreckers, 35, 50–51

Yellow fever, 14
Yamassee Indians, 42
Ylaco, 41